How to Get Your Wife to Cuckold You

A Cuckolding Guide for Cucks

and Cuck-Wannabes

By

Lionel Maximilien

Introduction

What does it take to be a cuckold in sex? And how do you get there without becoming a cuckold in your relationship and in life?

Becoming a cuckold is a one-way road. You may have already made steps towards it or just fantasized about it. This book will help you get there regardless while saving you from some common mistakes.

Once you cross the threshold and become a cuck for your wife, there is no turning back. You can't change your mind. Taking things from fantasy to a reality is a new beginning for both of you. If you feel ready to take that challenge then you want to be fully prepared for what is coming.

For many couples cuckolding brings them closer even though it can take some time for the wife to catch up with her husband's fantasy of her being with another man. Alternatively, a husband can take what seems like forever to admit that he isn't that good in bed and that another man would fulfill her more fully.

I have to make clear upfront that this guide is not erotica. This is a nuts-and-bolts guide to the process, pitfalls and hopefully, pleasures that you and your wife will face as you both work toward making your fantasies become a reality. If some of the language seems a bit dry that is because it is. Becoming a cuckold requires technique and knowledge. Sure we will talk about dildos, about cock locking and even bisexual cross-dressing cucks. But this is so that you are fully aware of your options., This book is here to help you make your cuck dreams become a reality without pain and minimum risk.

Some Terminology

Your name – that's cuck. Your wife's name is cuckoldress. The other man is typically referred to as a bull.

Cuckolding comes in a variety of levels. As a cuck you can be one of the types of men that prefer just to fantasize about your wife being with another man, or you could go as far as cleaning your wife's vagina after another man has cum in her. There is no limit to the cornucopia of sexual activities and identity roles that can be established between a couple when they are both ready and willing.

Bulls come in different types and shapes. We will cover these later when you need to find the right bull for your wife (and you). Meanwhile, it's important to get a firm grasp on exactly what your fantasy is. For some cucks, masturbating while thinking about your wife is enough. To know whether you want to take the fantasy to the next level or not, you should stop after you are done masturbating when you are completely spent and think about whether you want your wife to be with another guy or not. If the answer is still a resounding yes, then odds are, you are a cuck.

We all have fantasies that we play out in our imagination, but for many of us, the idea of going through with them is a stout no. Being a cuck, is much more than just sharing your wife with another man. Humiliation and being forced into a submissive role may work wonders for your sex life as a couple. The idea of being mentally, emotionally, and sometimes even physically tortured by their wife is the foundation of the fantasy.

Unfortunately, asking from your wife to switch from looking at you as the dominant sexual partner to thinking of your as the submissive one can be too much for her to handle. The good news is that with time, and the right strategy, you can increase your odds of getting your wife to cuckold you.

Why Cuckold to Begin With?

Most of the time a man becomes a cuckold without ever even trying to. One day he learns that his wife has been having an affair and he weighs out his options on what to do next about it. If he loves her deeply enough he may be willing to simply hold onto the relationship despite knowing that she is looking somewhere else to get her sexual needs fulfilled.

The degree of cuckolding is determined by how far she has gone with the other man. Is she only seeing him for sex? Odds are that she is also finding a certain degree of emotional and mental connection with the other guy. Many men will draw a line here and break up. For a cuck though, it is simply another hurdle that he must overcome to show his undying love for his cuckoldress.

Wanting to be a cuck isn't the signifier that you, as a man, are any less of a man. In fact, many of the men that find themselves in the position of preferring to be a cuck in the bedroom are men that are on top of the careers. Often, a cuck is a very intelligent man to the point of being headier when it comes to the things that turn him on. cucks are usually more into the fantasy aspect of sex and would prefer to allow their wives to be pleased by a bull that can take care of their wife sexually.

In many ways, being a cuck only outwardly shows that the man is in the submissive position. By giving up his daily identity as an executive powerhouse, the cuck is demonstrating that he is so confident in his ability to provide unwavering love for his wife that he can hand her over to another man. By allowing a bull to take over, the cuck may sense a certain aspect of control over the infidelity. Though, it is important (and we will discuss this later) that a cuck realizes that he isn't in control over whom the wife chooses to be the bull.

Part of playing out the cuck role is that all control over the sexual situation is completely lost. If the wife chooses to allow the cuck to take part in sex with her bull than it is up to her. She controls to what degree the cuck can achieve sexual satisfaction. Though, through this loss of control, the cuck will most certainly enjoy the emotional and physical torture of not being able to be dominant.

Is it Really Cuckolding?

Some will reportedly argue that simply by wanting your wife and discussing with her, the notion of cuckolding you are pulling away from the true definition of cuckolding. With such a potentially dangerous introduction to your lovemaking, does it fully matter on whether you initiate (no matter how subconsciously) your desire of being a cuck? Make no qualms, there is a distinct difference between being a cuck and just having a threesome. In a threesome, you are all three actively involved, with you playing a role that might be submissive, yet remaining equal.

In a cuckolding relationship, you are going to be left completely at a loss of control. Your wife gets to decide everything. From the bull that she chooses to whether you even know anything about it or not. Of course, you will know on your own that your wife is cheating on you but whether you get to know the details or not are completely up to her to decide. In this type of relationship, she may invite you to watch, or even decide to film it so you can watch later. Your role as a cuck is to essentially sit in the backseat of the relationship in term of sex. Don't expect things to ever go back to the way they were once you open this door.

For some men, like most people, they want to have their cake and eat it too. You might find that having your wife to love and support while watching her with another man is the perfect way to have everything you've ever wanted. Sometimes, knowing that another guy can give her all the things you can't sexually is a huge weight off your back. You no longer need to stress out about the fact that you can't please her sexually and you get to know that she is thoroughly having the time of her life. Just because it's not with you doesn't mean that she loves you any less, it just means she is a woman that knows how to please herself.

It is important to realize that there are several different types of cucks out there. The gradient of cuck experiences is much more of a spectrum than a simple definition. You may find yourself able and willing to travel the scale of cucking over time but will most certainly find yourself already on one side of the scale. Let us go over, in more detail, some of the different types of cucks. It's always good to know where you start before you open your fantasy up to your wife, should you choose to verbalize it to her. For some, letting her know would ruin the fantasy. Though you want to be a submissive cuck there's no set rules on when you draw the line. Be happy, and cuck on.

Types of Cuckolding

Rookies to cuckolding, play close attention to these next few sections. You need to know exactly where you stand in terms of what you want from the cuckolding affair. If you don't know your own limits from the start then how will you ever convince her of what you want?

Be aware, though, that many times a man starts off at one level of being a cuck only to lead into further developments of how far the fantasy goes. Sometimes, and you may be one of these cuck couples, the husband also has sex with the bull.

This is perhaps the ultimate level of being a cuck. Whatever your level on the spectrum of cuckolding, know that this fantasy is more common than you think.

The number of men that manage to convince their wives to go along with cuckolding is not high. However, with the help of some of the pointers I will give you, along with a further understanding of what you want from the experience, you will have much better chances to fulfill your fantasy.

The Classic Model Cuck

The traditional and classic model of a cuckold is one where the male doesn't necessarily get directly involved at all with the affair that is going on. For this type of cuckold there is no requirement to actually see his wife having sex with another man. The mere thought of her being the center of attention by another male is enough to stimulate the sort of longing that this level of cucking portrays.

For many men, cucking starts at this level and is a direct result of finding out that his wife has been cheating on him. By learning about how deviant she has been, the cuck finds himself to be the victim and is absolutely humiliated by the fact that he wasn't enough for his wife. Whether or not the cuck enjoys this position is absolutely beyond the wife's sense of empathy as she is already having the affair.

Guys that are at this stage of cucking tend to be more of the submissive type. This means that the woman doesn't just dominate in the bedroom, she also controls other issues of power, such as money and any major life decisions in the relationship. It's not unusual for a guy at this beginning stage of cuckolding to go along with the submissive position because he feels that he is no better than any other man and knows that he is unable to fulfill his wife's sexual needs. Eventually, he learns that the only way he is going to be able to keep her as a wife is to go along with the affair.

It is also important to realize that many times the wife at this stage will also do as much as she can to deny her husband of any sexual pleasure. She already has moved on to bigger and better (at least better) sex with somebody else. If he want's to maintain the marriage for whatever purposes his only option is to silently bite the bullet and let her take it from whomever she chooses.

It is natural even for the cuck to wonder why his wife is cheating on him. Is it because he is boring, is it because he has a small penis, or is simply because she wants to prove that she is the dominant one in the relationship? Regardless, the cuck is left to figure that out on his own.

Eventually, this stage, for almost every cuck, develops into a more sexually satisfying experience – to sit back and fantasize about his wife with somebody else. His imagination takes over and drives him mad with desire if he can truly enjoy being the submissive one in the marriage.

The Loving and Willing Model Cuck

Since you are reading this you have, more than likely, already reached this stage of cuckolding. This model of cuck is the type of husband that fantasizes constantly about his wife having sex with other men. He might have also attempted talking her into it. This type of cuck clearly knows where he stands in terms of being teased and ridiculed by his wife having sex with another man.

He loves it when she comes home and divulges all of the juicy details of the sordid love affair that she just had. He then goes to the bathroom and shamefully masturbates without her, because she probably wouldn't agree to him actually deriving sexual pleasure from the activity. She may, however, grant him the ability to have an orgasm. This type of cuck is deeply turned on and aroused by the fact that his wife just went and had sex with another man. He feels that she has absolute sexual power over him and would not even consider it to be any other way. When she returns home from her affairs is usually when this type of cuck feels the most intense sense of arousal.

An important aspect of the willing cuck is the fact that the two remain equals in the relationship when outside of the bedroom.

8

Their sexual roles are where they strip off the masks (or put them on) and get to explore their deepest and darkest fantasies. The highest majority of these cucks are husbands that exhibit some sort of executive control or at least hold high-power positions in the workforce. They have a large sense of duty and responsibility in their daily lives and therefore enjoy it when their wives take over and wield the reigns when it comes to sex. This way, they know for sure that their wives aren't sexually being neglected in their absence.

While this type of cuck is the most common and is comfortable with being submissive to his wife, he typically just enjoys watching and masturbating in the corner. He may even prefer to watch from another room, like through a peephole for instance. He can also enjoy filming it so that he can watch it later and then relive the fantasy over and over. This type of cuck, at this level, has no desire to actively be part of the intercourse with the bull. That's the next model.

The Pansy Model Cuck

Not every man reaches this level of cucking. This is when the cuck gets to explore his feminine side. He may go so far as to wear ladies' underwear, pantyhose, bras and even makeup. He looks forward to being thoroughly humiliated by the bull being with his wife. His wife may go so far as to take a ruler out and show her husband exactly how much he doesn't measure up to the large penis of the other man. Women with cucks of this nature often seek out bulls that are extremely masculine and well-endowed. This results in a complete opposite archetype than that of her Pansy Model cuck.

This model of cuck also has clearly expressed his desire to be a part of the sexual affair. Only, instead of being with his wife, he wants to be with the bull. He may participate by letting the wife use a strap-on or dildo while the bull makes the cuck give him a blowjob.

This cuck becomes the center of attention in many ways, as the wife and the bull completely emasculate the cuck and use him for their own pleasure. This could be through oral activities or even anally. As one can naturally anticipate, when you are talking about the Pansy Model cuck, the wife controls all parts of the relationship. She is completely, hands-down the most dominant one of the marriage. She will dish out the orders, and he will follow them.

Not every man that experiences the different levels of cucking will work his way up to being a Pansy Model. This degree of humiliation is simply not for everybody. For starters, there has to be a bisexual element. The bisexual element of cucking can often times surface at a later time. Eventually, he may start to wonder what it is like to be with Mr. Sexually Perfect. It's this form of idolization that can awaken any latent bisexual curiosities that the Pansy cuck may inhibit.

It is also important for all the cucks to realize that just because you have bisexual tendencies and may fantasize about being with another guy at the same time as you are your wife, that doesn't automatically make you a Pansy Model. It could just mean that you are bisexual. The humiliation aspect and the dressing up as a woman are typical indicators of the Pansy Model.

Moreover, not all Pansy Models are bisexual. Just because they like to wear makeup, wigs and woman's lingerie in the bedroom, they could still be straight as an arrow. There are no limits to what you are capable of exploring when you and your partner are communicating openly.

Across the Board

There are several similarities that seem to be the norm across the board in terms of defining the stereotypical cuck. You may find that you don't fit into any of these categories, but the reason they are here is to let you know that if you find yourself in any of them, you should know that you aren't alone. It's more, much more common than you think it is.

One of the first things that most cucks have in common is a penis obsession. They just can't get the thought of their penis size out of their head. They may always be looking for ways to increase the size or possibly they have just accepted that they have an average or smaller than average penis. More often than not, though, they will constantly be fixated on the fact that there is no way that their penis could please their wife. We'll touch on this later, but let's just say right now, you are probably just imagining things. Your dick is probably perfectly fine. Quit whining about it, cuck. Moving on now.

The next thing that seems to run across the board for all cucks is that they prefer to think about sex than actually do the deed. They spend so much time wrapped up in their fantasy land that they have grown accustomed to the landscape and simply prefer not to leave the perfect land of their imagination. cucks have a tendency to run more on the intellectual side and also have deep feelings and emotions that they may not have an active outlet for. This is one of the reasons that the idea of being a cuckold is so arousing. It provides the perfect combination of being mentally stimulated while also allowing the cuck to sit back and enjoy masturbating and fantasizing about what it would be like to give their wife the pleasure that the bull is able to provide.

Many cucks tend to have lower testosterone than the bull does. The bull will be the type that is able to get hard at the drop of a hat and keep it up for hours on end if that is what the cuckoldress wishes, and usually, it is.

cucks always prefer to be in the submissive position in the bedroom. There is a lot of argument among cuck communities on whether or not a person is a true cuck, or if they are just somebody that enjoys sex with multiple partners. In the end, there are no hard rules. If you want to call yourself a cuck, then call yourself a cuck. Just realize that for many people it means that the wife is in total control over the sexual situation, leaving you to sit back and watch or participate, if she allows it of course.

The final commonality among cucks is that they tend to be the type that would more readily spend hours of the day just thinking about their wives having an affair and feeling completely humiliated by it. It's this sort of emotional and psychological torture that the cuck puts himself willingly through that is the height of the fantasy. The moment of orgasm is hardly the thing that a cuck thinks about. Instead, he is thinking of his wife getting all the pleasure she could ever imagine. Those are thoughts that control the true cuck and his mind.

Oh Yeah, the Bull

We wouldn't want to leave the bull out of the situation now, would we? Though he is certainly not the cuckolding type, he is not always necessarily the big burly guy that you may imagine. In fact, he may have a penis that is just as comparable, even smaller than yours. The main thing to remember about the aspect of the bull is that there is generally some degree of humiliation that goes along with why your wife has chosen him to be the bull. Or, in fact, she could have just found him attractive and the very principle that she has cheated on you with him is enough to strip down your sense of manliness and make you feel like a submissive cuck. So, essentially the term bull

12

just is a common word referring to the man that is giving your wife the sex of her life. He could be the manager at the grocery store or the young college dude that works at the record store for minimum wage. Often times though he is a man that you already know or have already heard your wife talking about. She will often if the affair is already going on, hint at him before the cuckolding starts.

This is her way of testing the water, and also seeing how much you care (or don't care) about her constant talking of him. That co-worker that she refers to as her 'work husband' could just possibly be doing more than giving her hand at work. Think about that for a second, or a couple hours if you prefer.

Starting With Suggestion

One of the safest ways to get your wife to cuckold for you is to merely start with the power of suggestion. The suggestions that you offer in the beginning should be as basic and simple as you can make them, or else you might make your wife think that you are the one that is cheating on her. Imagine you stepped into the house and asked her if it would be a good idea for her to find another man to satisfy her sexual needs. She will immediately become suspicious of you and rightly so. Try to make your suggestions subtle. Start off by merely alluding to the fact that there are other fish out there in the sea.

This tactic can start just as easily from your home couch as it would from a trip to the local convenience store. The goal is to get her to begin to realize that other men are out there, and to start the conversation about what it would be like if she were with another man. If you are at home and watching television you could ask her which movie star she would choose if she could have sex with anybody. She may play coy at first and pretend that she really doesn't fantasize about anybody, but don't give up. Keep prying her. Tell her that you are sure there must be somebody. Tell her it could be a star that she used to fantasize about before she met you.

Sooner or later she is bound to give up the details. After she tells you, you have two options on how you can psychologically play the situation. The best is to get her to tell you why she thought the guy was hot, or what the sexual fantasy was about. This puts her mind in the position of thinking about somebody other than yourself. After you have accomplished this you should let the conversation fall away and move to a different topic for a while.

Then after a couple days have gone by, tell her that you saw the actor in a movie or in an article on the internet and that you can see why she finds him attractive. Don't compare yourself to him. Ask her to tell you about the fantasy once again. You can make slight comments that kid her about it, then ask her if there is anybody in her real life that she thinks would be just as good in bed.

Odds are she is just going to say no. After all, what woman or person for that matter, would actively admit to their partner about the fact of being attracted to another person? You will have to work at this technique for some time. Consider it to be the very beginning of a series of tactics that you will have to work toward to get her to go along with your dream of cuckolding. You are essentially laying down the groundwork that you are always going to be there for her and that the thought of her being with another man is just simply not something that would make you leave her. You have to be very careful at this stage too. You don't want to scare her off.

Another way that you can begin working through the power of suggestion is to take her to a public place where you can comment on complete strangers as the two of you go about your shopping or whatever it is you are doing. All you have to do is tell her that you just saw a guy looking at her. Get her to start to see that other men out there are paying attention to her.

Then if you are capable of it, take her someplace where you can buy her something for herself that will make her feel beautiful. Be sure to get your wife something that she actually wants and likes. Sure you might like the sexy lingerie, but if it's perfume and lotions that really make her feel sexy then you are going to have to swallow your own desire and give her what she wants. You need to get used to the feeling of her being in total control anyway.

Once the two of have spent some time out and about you can come home. It is time to get the suggestive seeds you planted early to sprout. Now is when you start to ask her if she ever thought about being with another guy. Ask her about the guy that was looking at her while you were at the mall. Ask her if she would do him if she were single.

Just like with the previous scenario of the 'free ride movie star', you probably won't get an answer out of her really quickly, at least not an honest answer. But with a little time and persuasion, you will. The important thing about these two little exercises, especially pointing out that another man was looking at her, is that you are starting to get her to do two things. The first is that she is starting to mentally picture what it would be like to be with another guy besides you. The second is that hopefully, she is starting to see herself in a new more attractive light.

After you have been with a person, sometimes for even a short period of time, it is easy to begin to lose that sense of attractiveness that helped bring the two of you together in the first place. When she is thinking about another man looking at her, she starts to realize that it would be possible to be with whoever she chose. Some women have this sense of confidence already hardwired into them, others need a little help to get the tiger to come out.

If your wife is the first type, then you are lucky. Getting her to want to cuckold might not be such a hard journey for you. If your wife is the second, lacking in confidence, you will have a much harder time. Even after you get her to see her true allure to other men, you will have to work harder as she learns to assert herself in the bedroom.

Turn the Tables

Once you have established that there are men in your wife's life that she finds attractive, and that they also find her attractive, you have completed the first step. The next thing that you need to do is flip the script and go from being the supportive and curious husband to the jealous and insecure husband.

While you are certainly employing some mind games that will be difficult to come back from, remember you are also looking to make a shift in your sexual relationship with her that could potentially change the scope of your relationship for the rest of your lives.

To show that you are jealous of the other men start begging for sex from her. Tell her that you need to know that she wants you, ask her if you are big enough, if your lovemaking is enough to please her. Ask her if she has ever really had an orgasm from you. Then the next big secret that you need to employ is to make the other guys look like "bad boys".

It's long been known that women often fall for the 'bad boy' type, but will often marry the 'good guy' just because he is more reliable and secure in the long run. Once you begin to tap into the primal urges that she secretly has to be with the bad boy in the bedroom the closer you become to being able to fulfill your cuckolding fantasy.

Whenever a guy hits on her, or she mentions that she finds one attractive, make a big deal about how wrong that guy would be for her. Point out that he looks like he spends his money on trying to have the best of everything, or tell her he looks like the type of guy that just uses women for sex. Remind her that he would never be able to give her the type of love that you give her.

This is when she will, no matter how subconsciously, begin to imagine what it would be like to be with the other man. She will begin to have a fantasy in her mind of being with the bad boy type which is going to be an opposite fantasy of what it's like for her to be with boring, old and routine you.

Beyond the Bad Boy

You don't have to rely necessarily on whether or not your wife is only in need of finding the typical 'bad boy' scenario. There are many reasons why a woman chooses to be with one guy over another. She may have developed some form of emotional attraction or the lust that she feels toward the other guy could stem merely from some old fantasy of hers. The point is, that unless you have open communication with her prior to her sexual encounter with the other guy, you won't necessarily know the reasons behind the affair.

For many married couples, the notion of cuckolding doesn't really enter the ballgame until well into their thirties and even as late as their early forties. At this age, the wife has begun to reach her sexual peak while at the same time the husband is typically starting to wane in his sexual desire. Even if he still has a fairly high sex drive, the wife is usually finally able to enjoy some of the most physical aspects of sex. This essentially means that this is the time of your wife's life when she is geared to have more sex than ever before.

Knowing that your wife is at your peak gives you the opportunity to fulfill your cuckolding fantasies by starting to talk to her about what it would be like to be with another guy. The idea that your wife has only ever thought about you is as silly and imaginary as the Easter Bunny. She's surely had thoughts, and who knows, she could have already acted on some of them behind your back. If you can get her to open up about what she wants and seeks in a man then you can also begin to discuss with her your exact standpoints.

One of the most important things that you can stress at this point is the strength of the marriage and love that you feel for her. If you can get her to realize that you wouldn't be jealous if she cheated on you and that it would, in fact, turn you on a bit, you start to peel away the false notions of what couples typically expect from one another.

The idea that when you get married to a person you are only going to sexually be with them, and only them, for the rest of your life together is, unfortunately, the byproduct of cultural and societal traditions and standards of the norm that are undeniably false. While some couples may be able to uphold the tradition of monogamy, how many of them are truly happy couples? Surely there are some, but most couples discover sooner or later that they get to set their own rules especially in regard to sex.

Once a couple is able to cross this threshold it is like a big curtain has been pulled back and the truth of the love that they feel for one another is open and flowing. There is no doubt that for some couples, having any sort of affair would be the signal for the end of a relationship. But, if the two of you are able to forgo on jealousy and intimidation, and instead focus on the beauty of being able to explore your sexual identities together (albeit with another male) then you are on the way to enriching your lives and yourselves.

Many men, instead of being confronted with jealousy when they find their wives with another man, they are in fact filled with a deep sense of pride. Not to objectify wives, but the feeling is similar to showing off your new Ferrari. While some men wouldn't ever dream of letting another guy drive his new Ferrari, others take a certain thrill in it. Perhaps the biggest thrill is that no matter how often another guy may drive the car, it's never actually going to be his. Call this a far stretch for many, but the biological factor that occurs when a man watches another guy go at it with his wife is a thrill that makes him want her more.

Scientists have done many studies to try and figure out why there is such a growing trend among men wanting to cuckold for their wives, and the truth is the trend isn't new at all. Men have been enjoying cuckolding for as long as relationships have been around. The difference is that now, with the added privacy that internet chat rooms provide, individuals and couples are able to be more open and form communities of like-minded people without having to give up personal information.

The scientific approach suggests that a man feels a rise in competition when he sees another man having sex with his wife. Biologists, anthropologists, and theorists suggest that there is essentially a sperm battle going on. When there is the presence of another man's sperm other guys want to make their own sperm present too. It's an evolutionary factor that happens on such a subconscious level, most men aren't fully aware of why it is so sexy to fantasize about their wife with another man.

Essentially this means that even though you are being the more submissive one, by allowing your wife to be used by another man in bed, there is an underlying motivation which revolves more around you being the alpha male. After all, it is your wife that the another man is getting it on with. At the end of the day, he goes on about his way and you are left behind to dominate with your own sperm.

Let Her Set it Up

Regardless of biological factors which may motivate you to want to let another man enter your wife, you don't get to be the one that sets it up. Sure, it seems like a good idea to invite your best buddy to bunk up with your wife, but if she isn't attracted to him then it is not going to work. You can do your best to persuade her through suggestive language toward the type of guy that would turn you on to see her with, but at the end of the day, the choice is completely hers.

You may have somebody in mind, like the boss that you have at work that is a complete jerk and drives the car you wish you had and has a wife that you know is hotter than yours. The drive to compete against this man and prove that you are better by having something (your wife) that he desires could be just the sort of thing you need to get your blood pressure up in more ways than one.

As mentioned earlier there are about as many different reasons and types of cuckolding scenarios as there are flavors of ice cream. The important thing is that in each scenario the wife always gets to choose who she is going to be with. The ultimate thing that should result from the cuckolding is that your wife is sexually satisfied by another dude. If she isn't getting pleased then the scenario gets turned around into her essentially doing you a favor by acting out a fantasy for you.

The person she ends up choosing may infuriate you to the point of no return. Use this sort of resentment to help fuel your desire as you watch your wife take it from some low-life scum. Who knows what type of guy (or guys) that she will end up with once you finally let her know that you are going to love her no matter what.

If You Have a Friend in Mind

If there happens to be a friend of yours that you have in mind for the cuckolding experiment then you have to be really tricky about introducing the thought to your wife. You can't exactly say, "Hey, why don't you sleep with our friend Bob?" Well, you could say that, but you wouldn't really be working the notion of using any sort of psychological prowess to get her to be doing it with him. You need to make her think of him as the bull and to get her to do that there are a couple techniques that you can employ.

For starters, you can begin talking about all the different things that Bob (we'll stick with that name) has that you don't have. If Bob has a head full of hair, ask your wife if she thinks you are balding. If Bob has big muscles, ask your wife if she thinks your arms are scrawny and sissy like. She will probably tell you (any good wife would at least) that you are perfectly fine the way you are. But what you are really doing is starting to put the thought into her head that Bob is better than you. Then the next step where you really set off the power of suggestion is to have Bob over.

Be sure that you have already talked to Bob a bit so that he is aware what you are up to. Remember, this is the scenario where you have the perfect guy already in mind. Let your wife hear the two of you at some sort of verbal battle, or even play some sort of competitive sport where she can see how much you suck compared to the near-perfect Bob. Let your friend win every competition. Whatever it is that you choose to do, just make sure that your wife is well aware of the fact that Bob has swagger and you don't. With time, and a little flirting on his behalf coupled with you asking your wife constantly about being with other men, you will likely lead the two into the arms of each other. Then let the cuckolding commence.

Into Action

Once things get underway in your new relationship with her as your cuckoldress you will feel like you have arrived at a new place that you need to explore even further. The main difference that most women go through, is a shift in how dominant they are throughout other aspects of their life besides the bedroom. As your wife experiences her sexual liberation you can anticipate that other dynamics between you will change as well. Now that you have encouraged her to be more empowered you should be prepared for what is to come.

Attention Hound

Remember those days when you were able to do something simple like bring her a flower or even buy her some candy to make her day a little sweeter? Yeah, those days are going to be long gone. Now that cute little gift that you used to give her will make her think of all the other gifts that she is being bestowed upon from other suitors. You can make a safe bet that whoever she chooses to be her bull, he is probably giving her a little more than just sex. Many times the wife in a cuckolding relationship will go so far as to have actual date nights with the bull before they get to the sex part of the relationship. When this starts to happen to you, you will have to raise your gift-giving and affectionate attention to the next level. It's not just your sperm that is in competition at this point. You have to make sure that no matter what she is receiving from the bull she knows and fully understands that you are her husband and love her deeper and more fully than any other man possibly could. You already swept her off her feet once, you can surely maintain it. Even if another man is occasionally knocking her socks off.

More Demanding

As she gets more comfortable in her role as dominant she will start to learn that she is certainly worth all of the attention that she is getting. With this comes the added cost of the fact that she will become even harder to please. Not just romantically, but also in conversation. Her demands will likely increase now that she knows she is free to sleep with whomever.

For many men that wish to be cuckolded by their wives, there is a large amount of putting her up on a pedestal that is far beyond the normal amount of 'wife worship' that most men have. From this position, many men that want to be cucks are able to justify, and actually want, their wives to be in the dominant position in all aspects of their life.

When she starts arguing over who took the trash out last or telling you to do your own laundry, you know that you have entered into that phase of cuckolding when she is totally standing up for herself. This can make the marital relationship a little strained at times, but if you truly want to allow her to be dominant then you need to stand by her as she works through these new surges in assertive power.

Her sense of self-value is on the rise. She will start thinking that she is worth whatever it is she may want at the time. From having the steak for dinner to eating the last piece of anything she wants, she will make sure that she gets what she desires. This is the perfect place for her to be in regarding her cuckolding you. When she is assertive like this, it lets you know that she really is enjoying herself sexually and that she isn't just doing it to fulfill your own fantasy. Watching her get mind-blowing pleasure from another man is just the sort of thing a true cuck is after. Fasten your safety belt when your wife gets to this stage of the game.

More From You

Along with demanding more from every aspect of life, your wife will also want to have more from you too. Forget about sitting around talking about all the things that you want to do with your life. You will have to get up and do them. Perhaps you already are an Alpha male that gets things done without being told so. But if you are not, be prepared for her to have far less patience with you. For some men, that like to be cuckolded this is exactly the sort of 'punishment' that they feel they deserve.

You may also find it annoying that she is no longer the passive-aggressive person that she used to be. Trust that as she continues to get more comfortable in her role in cuckolding she will also expect you to be able to match her assertiveness. Sure, she may take the reigns in the bedroom from now on, but she will still expect you to be the man in the traditional sense and be able to provide for her. Only now, instead of providing what she needs you will have to give her what she wants. She'll let you know, one way or another.

Don't be surprised if you start sensing that she really doesn't need to have you around anymore. Her growing self-confidence is likely to translate to growing self-sufficiency which means less dependence on you.

This growth can be challenging but is also beyond a doubt a turn on for a cuck. Watching a woman go from being homely and docile (if that is the type of wife you currently have) to becoming an alpha-woman is certainly a major transformation. Her transformation is likely to be permanent as she grows more and more liberated and in touch with giving herself.

The Enigma

You should expect your wife to start to become more and more of a mystery to you. Odds are that when she lets out her sexy tiger she will continue with unleashing a fury of dominance that you never imagined she had. Don't be surprised when she starts withholding information from you in regard to her sexual encounters. She will grow into being the one that decides how much information you get to know and when you get to know it. This, after all, is the truest definition of being a cuck for her. You don't get to make any of the decisions anymore. The enigma that is now a fully independent woman is a mystery for any man.

Clearly, as a woman, she thinks much differently than you. Before you know it she might have you tied up in the corner and blindfolded. You won't be able to touch yourself or even see what is going on, but you will be surrounded (if she chooses) by all the different sounds and smells of her and her lover together.

The further you get into the lifestyle the higher the reward of watching her with other men will become for the both of you. Also, as she learns more about your growing (literally) pleasure of watching her with another man she will begin to control it. That is if you have set up the groundwork to build her into a truly dominating and controlling cuckolding master.

She will make sure to keep you on your toes in terms of what to expect. Men may think about sex constantly, but it's the women that truly have the highest sense of imagination and fantasy. Your wife will be able to come up with scenarios that are constantly challenging her sense of freedom and how much you are willing to give up control.

The more you encourage her with your unwavering faith and devotion to her, the more she will feel comfortable to let you in on some of her wildest and sluttiest fantasies imaginable. Keep her happy and highly worshiped and you will be on the highway to a wild and kinky sex life.

Playing the Victim

No matter what degree of cuckolding you are partaking in you will eventually begin to lead yourself into playing the role of the 'victim'. This may be the furthest of your intentions in the beginning, especially after you have put all the effort into trying subliminally, or bluntly, to get your wife to want and actually have sex with another guy. You are playing out the submissive role by giving up your dominance in the bedroom. She gets all the control right down to deciding whether or not you will even get to come.

Many couples take this a step further and the wife actually puts a chastity belt, or a penis lock, on her husband so that she is in total control over whether he gets to have an orgasm or not. She may even make you whip out your cock and compare it to the other man just so that she can get the opportunity to fully humiliate you next to him if his penis is larger. For many men, that want to be cuckolded this is all part of actualizing the role of being submissive. They want to be humiliated as a way of addressing any shortcomings that they may have in the bedroom. Because they are not able to make their wife feel good enough in the bedroom they get the pleasure of sitting back and watching another man take over the reigns.

Plus, there is certainly a degree of obsession over the size of their own penis. Many men that enjoy playing this role in the bedroom spend a lot of time thinking about how their penis compares to the size of other men. Sometimes a guy's penis can be perfectly fine (and usually guys, your penis is perfectly fine) but yet still they believe that their dick isn't quite big enough. One can blame this easily on the horse-hung men that are actors in porn.

Many times the industry uses a large amount of camera angle tricks along with other directorial choices, such as using a small woman with an average sized man, to make the male's penis look larger. From a young age, men are constantly taught that having a large penis equates to being a better man. They also believe that women truly want to have sex with a larger penis. In all reality, most women prefer so many other aspects of the lovemaking process, that the size of a man's penis is hardly the first thing on her mind. Unless of course, it is too big which can cause much more pain than pleasure.

This is another reason why you should let your wife be in total control over who she chooses to cuckold you with. Just because you might think she wants the gym ape with the 9-inch penis as thick as a soup can doesn't mean that she really does. She would probably prefer the man that actually knows how to work with what he's got. You may be able to take a few lessons from him as you watch the two of them together. You never know what you might learn.

The End Result

After your wife and you have entered into the realms of letting another male into your bedroom, you will have to face the reality of what you have done to your marriage.

For some couples, their marriage is strengthened in a way that most traditionalists could never imagine. Considering that monogamy is one of the cornerstones of a marriage, breaking it with infidelity begins to break down some of the foundation that the marriage was built on.

Dream Scenario

There is the ideal scenario where everything works out perfectly fine and the two of you are able to actively play out your fantasies with one another. Your wife enjoys the sexual pleasure that she is receiving along with the new found role of being dominant while you prefer to take a back seat and play the role of victim. For all of the scenarios that the two of you play out, you never get a sense of jealousy. If you do the feeling brings on a sense of arousal as opposed to being truly upset. The trauma of watching your wife with another man can be intense regardless of how much you have fantasized about it and wanted it to happen.

In the perfect world, the two of you will be able to act out various sexual roles and still maintain respect for one another. Some of the men that take cuckolding to the highest level and are actually engaging in sexual activities with the bull as well, may find that their wife actually likes watching her husband suck her vaginal juices off from another guy's penis. If everybody is happy with what they are doing then what could be the harm?

If you find yourself blessed with such an open and adventurous wife then you are in a prime position to keep exploring as long as the two of you remain happy. Open communication is one of the best ways to make sure that neither of you is hurt from your redefined relationship.

When It Has Gone Too Far

If your wife is consistently cuckolding you with the same bull there is more than a fair chance that she will eventually develop feelings for him. This may happen quickly as most women rely on a heightened emotional and mental connection to help them achieve sexual pleasure.

When this occurs you can basically kiss your marriage goodbye. If your wife is able to keep these feelings in check then you should just be forewarned that you are certainly playing with fire. After all, she is falling in love with another guy. And once love starts to come into the picture, you have a wedge forming in your marriage.

If another man is able to pry the two of you apart, and there are feelings involved between the two of them, then a divorce is more than likely the outcome of exploring your cuckolding fantasy. In fact, it doesn't matter whose fantasy it was, to begin with. Whether she deviated from your marriage and you found out she was cheating on you or you were the one that suggested it to her, when she falls in love with the other guy you can't blame yourself.

There is no way of stopping two people from falling in love. If she has gone so far as to start feeling emotions for the bull, would you really want to perpetuate your victim role further by staying with a woman that is no longer in love with you? It may seem like something you can do for a little while, but at the end of the day, you should be aware that deserve a woman that who will always return to you and not the bull.

After essentially giving her the go ahead that it is okay with you if she is with another man, you would think that she would respect you more, but often times it leads to the opposite and the wife soon is swooning over someone else. She just might not tell you until your bags are packed for you and they are waiting on the front stoop when you get home from work, the sounds of her lovemaking screaming from what used to be your bedroom too. Be smart and practice open communication. If you demand anything out of the situation, demand that.

The Building Resentment

It might have nothing to do with her falling in love with the bull when she tells you that she wants a divorce. Sometimes when you open doors that weren't already open for you, you invite unwanted guests into your home. This is the case with any resentments that may form as a result of the cuckolding experience. Think about it for a second. Your wife has gone from seeing you as the master of her universe, her king, her master, to seeing you as her little bitch.

Her opinion of you is likely to change considerably after you make it clear you are into watching her take it from another man. For some women, this may be empowering, but for many, they are simply doing it to help you along with the fantasy that you have told them about. If your wife is going along with you just to keep you turned on and happy then you can bet that she will start building resentment. She may simply begin to be upset that you would jeopardize your marriage with her by even considering infidelity despite the fact that it is on her side. It is possible that in her eyes you are objectifying her by getting her to be a living prop in your sexual fantasy.

So what do you do if this is the case? First off remind her how beautiful she is and remind her that you would never want her to do anything that she wasn't comfortable with. Tell her that you know that other guys are after her and that it wouldn't bother you that much if she gave in to her desires. It has to be perfectly clear to her that you aren't objectifying her. She needs to know what a sex goddess she is and it's your responsibility to let her know.

If the resentment sets in it is still possible for you to pull yourself out of the spin. Just like a car accident you probably won't see it coming until it's too late, but if you do happen to pick up even the slightest hint that she really isn't into your fantasy, you have to be sure that you don't ridicule her. Don't call her uptight or prudish. Just let her know that you were kidding and continue to go on about your lovemaking with her.

The best time (if there ever is one) of letting her know about your secret fantasy of her cuckolding you is probably after you are done making love to her. Let her know that you are the luckiest man on the earth and that other guys would die to be with her. Remember, from earlier, that it's all about making her feel like the queen bee. For most men that like the notion of being the target of a cuckold experience, they already hold their wives in such a high position.

33

Telling her how any man should die to be with her should come as a natural sentiment.

If you can keep her feeling good about the intimacy that you already share with her then you can cut back on the damage that caustic resentments can form over time. You certainly don't want to revisit the idea until she brings it up again. When she does (and she probably will) be ready to be prepared with a nonchalant answer that makes it seem as if you really could care less about it anymore. You have done your job of planting the seed and now all you have to do is sit back and watch as she begins to take notice of what the other guys want.

Counseling

Counseling. Yep, that's one word that no man ever wants to hear come out of his wife's lips. Especially when it involves going to one because of a fantasy that he shared with her. But you should be well informed that many couples have explored what it is like to bring other partners into the bedroom. The outcome for many is, unfortunately, bleak in terms of maintaining the relationship.

You would be surprised at the number of couples that are going to counseling because of problems in the bedroom. Many times it's simply because they are unable to admit to their close friends what the degree of sexual exploration that they have undertaken. Some people are scared to talk about cuckolding because they think that other people will view them as loose or simply not dedicated to the same core values as other members of the community.

When this sort of pressure becomes apparent counseling can certainly help couples. Some married men would normally, and easily, talk over the water cooler about their latest sexual explorations. However, when it comes to playing out the role of a cuck, very few men are eager to brag to their friends about the humiliation that their wife made them go through over the weekend. Thankfully, for those cucks out there, the growing community of men that are coming out about these secret fantasies is growing. This makes avoiding counseling even easier when you have a few good friends to talk to. Keep in mind though that there is never a firm solid replacement for seeking a counselor that is trained in sex therapy.

For the trained professional it will be no big deal to discuss all of the reasons why you seek active humiliation in the bedroom or even why you feel the need to be a participant with the bull, even though you don't readily identify yourself as a bisexual man.

Counseling can also help rectify any resentments that your wife may have formed with you when you told her what you really wanted to do. The counselor will help your wife understand that this fantasy is a very common fantasy. She (or he) will let your wife know that it has no reflection on your love for her, and will, in fact, help open up lines of communication so that the two of you can grow and keep your marriage intact.

If you feel the need to see a counselor, don't be ashamed to let your wife know, but it most cases it seems as if the wife is the one that initially brings up meeting with a counselor. If your wife suggests that you see a counselor, you better do it. After all, you suggested she take it from another man. The least you can do is take an hour on a sofa with a counselor. And possibly, just possibly, she may begin to see things from your perspective, and you might just end up getting what you wished, to begin with.

Seeing a counselor is certainly not a way that you want to go about getting your wife to cuckold for you but it could be just the right way for her to understand that you don't see her as a dirty slut and that you actually love her and just want her to be more sexually fulfilled as well as more dominant in the bedroom.

One Final Note

One final thing that you should remember when you are trying to get your wife to cuckold you is that you are ultimately throwing your marriage on the line. Be prepared for all of what may happen once you do this. If you choose to go about using some of the techniques that we discussed that are more subliminal and psychological in nature, be prepared that you might be setting yourself up for disaster should she actually fall in love with another man and end up leaving you. You also need to realize that for many couples there are essentially two ways of getting your wife to cuckold for you.

The first one: she already is. In this scenario, the wife is already cheating on you and you have discovered (whether on your own or because she told you about it) that she is having an affair. The other means of entering into the cuckolding community is generally done simply through an open conversation with your wife. The two of you should be able to discuss anything.

Just remember, that you probably want to ease into the conversation, else the subject matter could hit her like a ton of bricks and have her buying a one-way ticket away from you. Generally though with a little bit of time and honest communication you can come to some sort of middle ground on what the two of you are willing to do.

Some men that enjoy the idea of being a cuckold but are with wives that simply will not go along, find that they can still turn to their fantasy through other means. Some men are able to get their wives to watch porn with them. This can be fulfilling for the cuck who can watch the man on the screen and pretend that he is the bull. However, this usually isn't quite enough for the wife-worshiping cuck that wants to make sure that his wife's needs are fulfilled. That's where the use of dildos can easily help out.

Also, just merely asking her what she wants and getting her to express her sexual desires could be enough to make you realize that you don't have to be a cuck after all. Perhaps you are quite capable of sexually fulfilling her every needs yet you just haven't begun to build the confidence, or let go of your own insecurities enough to realize that you are already her bull. Also, even if you are pleasing her thoroughly, you may be like many cucks, that simply want another man to do it so they can sit back and watch.

The human psyche and human sexuality are so intensely varied and unique to each person that it is hard to ascertain exactly what makes a cuck a cuck, and even harder to define how to get your wife to cuckold for you. The best way is always communication. Remember that. Good luck cucking!

Did you know you could leave an anonymous Amazon review?

If you enjoyed this book, and would like to help make cuckolding more understood and accepted, please consider leaving a review on Amazon.

https://www.amazon.com/dp/B01N33SKSW

If you are concerned about privacy, you can always use a pen name other than your name. You can change your pen name in a few seconds by following these video instructions:

https://www.youtube.com/watch?v=p5IrU3nPivs